Maple

APART

Lori Nichols

SCHOLASTIC INC.

For Elizabeth Vander Kamp, storyteller extraordinaire

Lori would like to thank Tressa and Cooper for their huge imaginations,
which sparked the idea for this story.

ISBN 978-1-338-28888-9

12 11 10 9 8 7 6 5 4 3 2 1 18 19 20 21 22 23

Printed in the U.S.A. 40

First Scholastic printing, September 2018

Design by Marikka Tamura
Text set in LTC Kennerley Pro
The illustrations for this book were rendered in pencil on Mylar and then digitally colored.

Maple and Willow loved summer.

And on the last day of summer,
the girls played together extra hard . . .

. . . because on Monday,
Maple was starting big-girl school.

Willow was a big girl, too . . .
but Willow was staying at home.

Home wasn't the same
without Maple.

When Maple came home,
she couldn't stop talking
about kindergarten.

"My teacher is so nice and I sat by a girl with curly red hair who has freckles and she's a twin and we played at recess. And it's going to be her birthday and she's going to have a party in our class . . ."

"I had fun, too," said Willow.
"I played with Pip."

"Pip?" Maple asked. "Who's Pip?"

"Pip is *my* new friend," said Willow.
"He has a bumpy head and he is afraid
of squirrels."

"We met by the oak tree."

On Tuesday, Willow explored
while Maple was at school.

Later, Willow heard all about kindergarten, again.

"We had story time in a circle and then went around the circle and everyone shared something special and I shared my heart rock since I had one in my coat pocket, and tomorrow we start learning the letters of our names . . ."

"Well, today, Pip and I played Rock School," Willow said. "I'm the teacher. I hide a rock in one of my hands. Pip moves up a grade each time he guesses which hand the rock is in."

"*Pip's in* third *grade!*"

After school on Wednesday, Maple couldn't wait to talk about her day.

"The playground has a fire engine with a steering wheel and monkey bars and a rocket slide, Willow. It was so much fun that we didn't want to stop for quiet time and my teacher had to tell us to put on our listening ears."

"I went to Pip's today," Willow said.
"He lives in a tree house."

"I've wanted a tree house forever," Maple said.

"I know," said Willow. "Me too."

"I can see our yard from Pip's tree house!"

The next morning,
Maple looked a little sad when
she said good-bye to Willow.

That afternoon, Maple was quiet.

"I rode with Pip today,"
Willow told her.

"You don't know how to ride,"
said Maple.

"Pip taught me," said Willow.
"We go slow."

"And we have loud horns!"

Beep! Beep!

"But I wanted to teach you
how to ride," said Maple.

"I know, but you're gone
a lot," said Willow.

"Willow, I like being at school," Maple said.
"But I miss playing at home."

The next morning,
Willow had a surprise for Maple.

"Maple, Pip wants to go to school with you today."

"Really?" Maple asked.

"Yes!" said Willow. "He's in your pocket."

At school, Maple introduced her friends to Pip.

And that afternoon, and all weekend long,
both girls played with Pip.

From then on, whenever Maple went to school, she brought Pip with her.

And that was okay with Willow, because Pip had a big family!